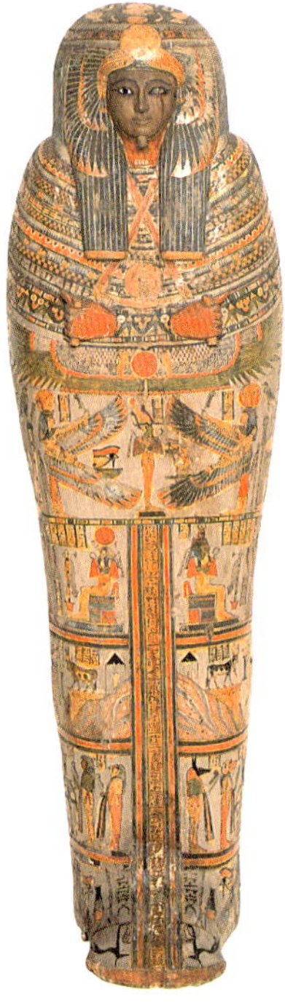

BRITISH MUSEUM POCKET TREASURY

Mummies

Egyptian mummies have an enduring fascination. The malevolent mummy of the 1930s 'horror film' may have little in common with the genuine article, yet over the centuries the treatment of ancient mummies has often been strange and grotesque: they have been ground to powder for use as medicaments, burnt as locomotive fuel, turned into wrapping paper, and 'unrolled' at social gatherings to satisfy the morbid curiosity of aristocratic travellers. Fortunately, since 1900 their value as a source of data about past populations has been generally recognised, and the ever-increasing arsenal of sophisticated imaging and analytical techniques has vastly increased their potential for broadening our understanding of the state of health, nutrition, life expectancy, diseases and ethnic affinities of the ancient inhabitants of the Nile Valley.

It was a fundamental tenet of ancient Egyptian religious belief that death was not the end of human existence. Rather, it was a transition, a necessity if one was to pass into the eternal afterlife in the realm of the gods. To reach this blessed state the three main components of the individual – the body and the non-physical *ka* ('life-force') and *ba* ('character' or 'personality') had to survive, to be reunited after death. The practice of mummification arose in response to the Egyptians' desire to preserve the corpse for eternity.

Great importance was attached to providing a tomb, as a safe resting place for the mummy and as the focal point for the making of offerings to the deceased. The tomb was stocked with a variety of funerary furnishings, including the coffin. This most important item served the deceased on many different levels – as an eternal dwelling, as a substitute for the body, or as a miniature version of the universe, roles which are repeatedly alluded to in the varied religious texts and images with which the surfaces of the coffins were covered. These coffins and the closely associated masks are in many ways more eloquent testimony to the ancient Egyptians' religious faith than are the mummies themselves.

'GINGER'

LATE PREDYNASTIC PERIOD *c.*3400 BC

'Ginger' (a modern nickname deriving from the colour of his hair) was buried in a small pit-grave scooped out of the desert sand at Gebelein in Upper Egypt. The hot, dry sand in direct contact with his body acted as an excellent natural preservative, and his hair, teeth, fingernails and skin have survived in remarkably good condition. Pottery and stone vessels, a mudstone palette, a flint knife and beads of 'Ginger's' time but found elsewhere have been placed around his corpse to illustrate the manner in which the dead were provided with basic necessities at this early date. In time, experiments were made to improve on natural preservation by artificial methods. This led ultimately to true mummification, involving the removal of internal organs, and the drying of the body with natron.

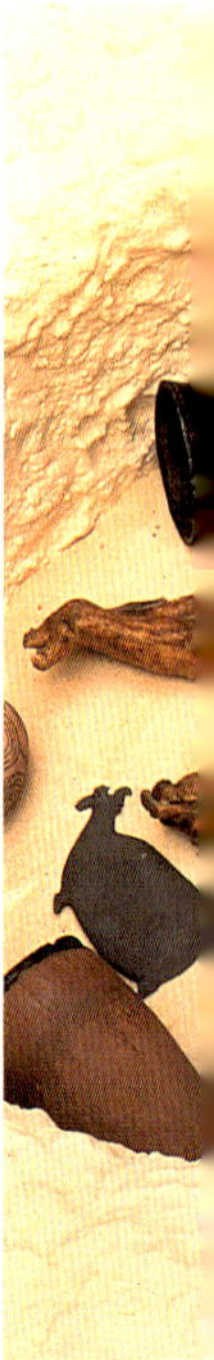

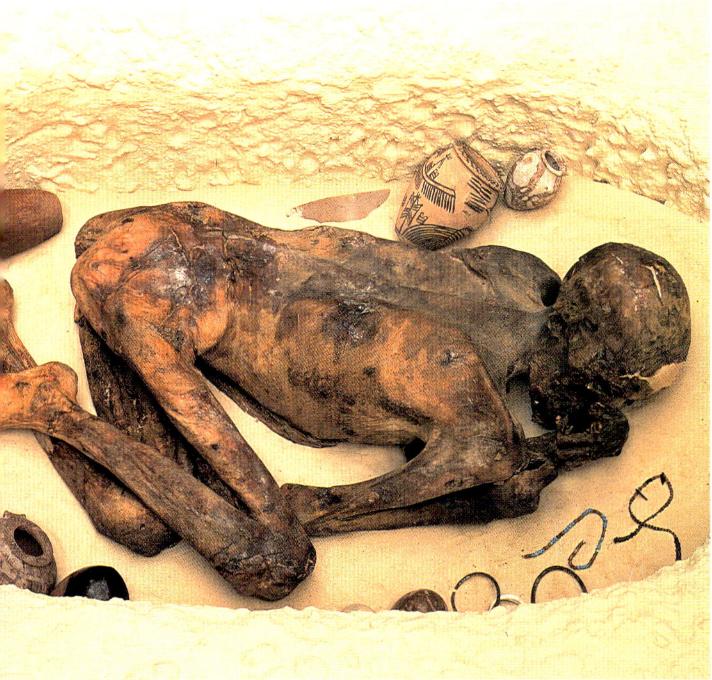

Wrapped Mummy of a Woman

Third Intermediate Period,

*c.*1069-664 BC

This mummy of an unidentified adult female can be dated to the Third Intermediate Period on the evidence of certain aspects of the embalming revealed by X-rays: artificial eyes placed in the orbits, and subcutaneous packing under the skin of the neck. The faience and beadwork scarab and cartonnage cover probably belonged to mummies of later date. The specimen also illustrates the appearance of a body with its wrappings intact.

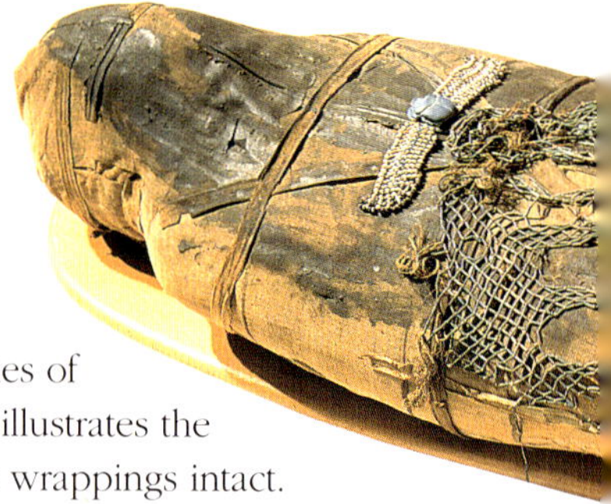

The practice of wrapping the body in linen cloths and bandages can be traced back to the Early Dynastic Period (early third millennium BC), predating the beginnings of true mummification in Egypt. Probably originally intended to maintain the physical integrity of the corpse, in the course of time the custom of wrapping it in linen acquired a symbolic significance, by helping to make the deceased a divine being. The *Ritual of Embalming*, a text preserved in copies from the Roman Period but probably reflecting much older traditions, provides details of the prescribed ritual acts which accompanied the wrapping stage. This text reveals that the outermost covers and binding tapes were envisaged as the garments of a warrior, which equipped the deceased to 'clear the way before Osiris' in the next world.

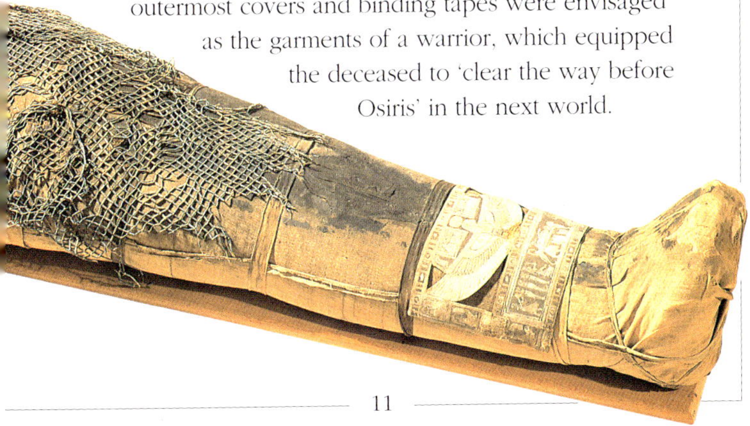

Mummy of Ankhef With Cartonnage Mask

Twelfth Dynasty, *c.* 1985-1795 BC

Beginning in the First Intermediate Period, about 2200 BC, an important part of the mummy's trappings was a mask that was placed over the head and shoulders during the final stages of wrapping. Early examples, such as this one still *in situ* on the mummy of Ankhef from Asyut, were made from cartonnage, a versatile medium consisting of layers of linen and plaster, pliable when soft, yet which hardened to produce a material that was both tough and lightweight. The large eyes and the stylised representation of facial hair are typical of the masks of the twenty-first-twentieth centuries BC. The magical function of the mask was to elevate the deceased from mortal status to that of divinity. Thus the face was covered with gold leaf (the gods were believed to possess shining golden skin) or, as here, given a less expensive coating of yellow paint.

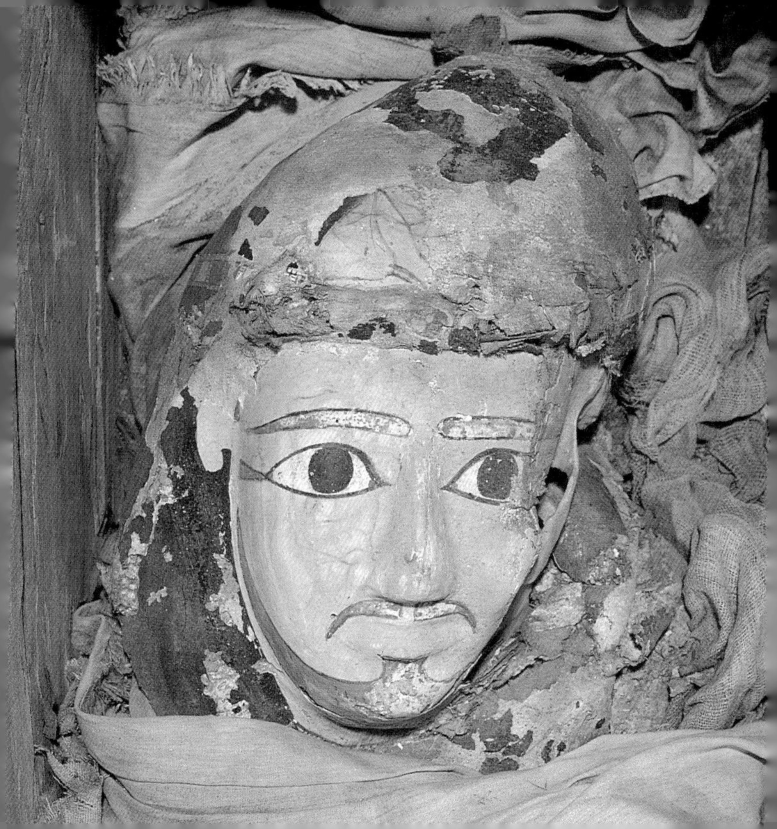

Coffin of Sepi

Twelfth Dynasty, c.1985-1795 BC

The earliest Egyptian coffins were rectangular in shape and were intended to be positioned in the tomb on a north-south axis with one long side facing east. The mummy within was laid on its side so that the deceased in his tomb on the west bank of the Nile could face the rising sun and look towards the world of the living. As a magical aid, two eyes were painted or carved on the eastern-facing side of the coffin, in alignment with the mummy's face. On this coffin of the General Sepi from El-Bersha in Middle Egypt, the eyes are located above a stylised doorway which enabled the spirit to pass freely in and out of the coffin to partake of his funerary offerings in the adjacent tomb chapel.

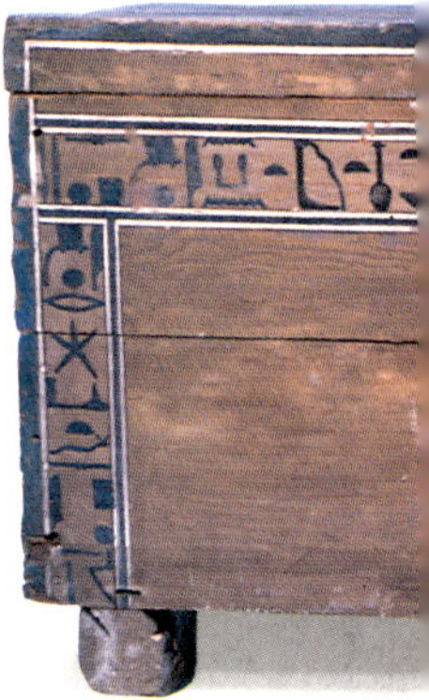

The horizontal inscription is a prayer to Osiris to provide food, drink, incense and 'all things good and pure' for the benefit of Sepi's *ka*. The vertical texts invoke the assistance of other gods, who were conceived as forming a protective ring around the deceased.

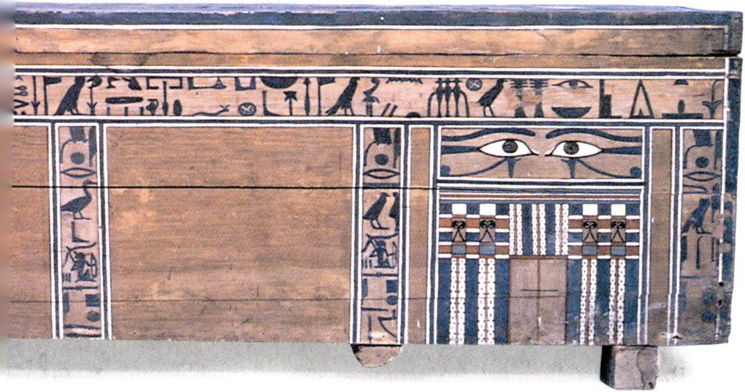

Head of the Coffin of King Intef

Seventeenth Dynasty, *c.* 1600 BC

This King Intef ruled southern Upper Egypt at a time when the Delta and the northern part of the Nile Valley were under the control of the Asiatic chieftains known as the Hyksos. He was buried at Dra Abu el-Naga in the Theban necropolis where his coffin and mummy were discovered by local diggers in 1827. The mummy unfortunately did not survive, though portions of the wrappings still adhere to the inside of the coffin. The coffin is made from the wood of the sycamore fig, a common tree native to Upper Egypt. The fact that Intef was unable to procure the more desirable cedar for his coffin is probably a reflection of the political situation in his reign, when southern Egypt was cut off from major trading routes through which fine timber could be obtained. The lid shows the king's body swathed in feathers, a style of decoration which has given rise to the modern term *Rishi* (from Arabic: 'feathered') for these coffins.

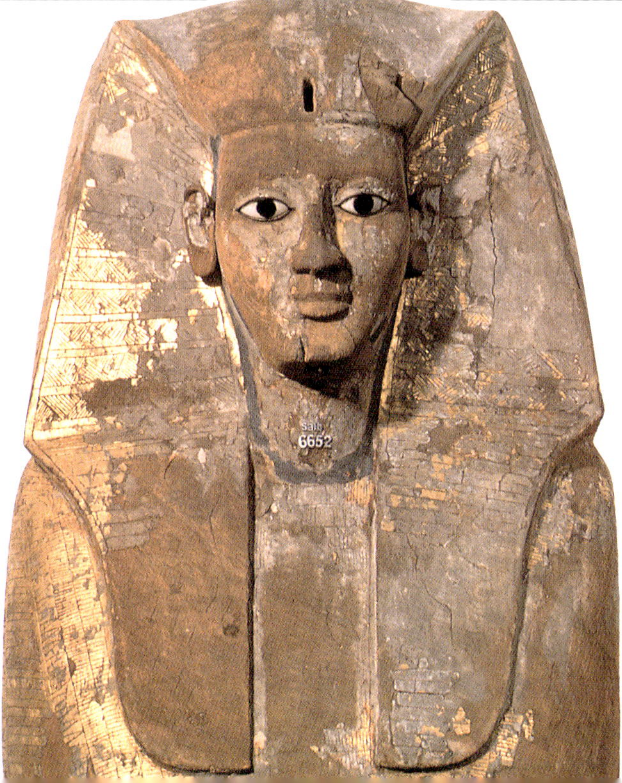
Salt
6652

Mummy Mask of the Lady Satdjehuty

Early Eighteenth Dynasty, *c.*1500 BC

The exquisite modelling of this cartonnage mask, together with the gilding of the face and headdress testifies to the importance of the lady for whom it was made. Her name is missing from the short offering formulae inscribed on the front, but hieroglyphic texts on pieces of linen from the same burial indicate that her name was Satdjehuty and that she enjoyed the favour of Queen Ahmose-Nefertary, wife of King Ahmose I. The colour scheme of the mask is characteristic of the funerary furniture of the early Eighteenth Dynasty, but the winged headdress is unusual on a mask of that period. It may be related to the feathered decoration of the *Rishi* coffins, which were still in use at this date. A possible alternative explanation is that the motif is a version of the 'vulture headdress', but since this was normally depicted being worn only by goddesses and female members of the royal family its presence on the mummy of a private individual would be unusual.

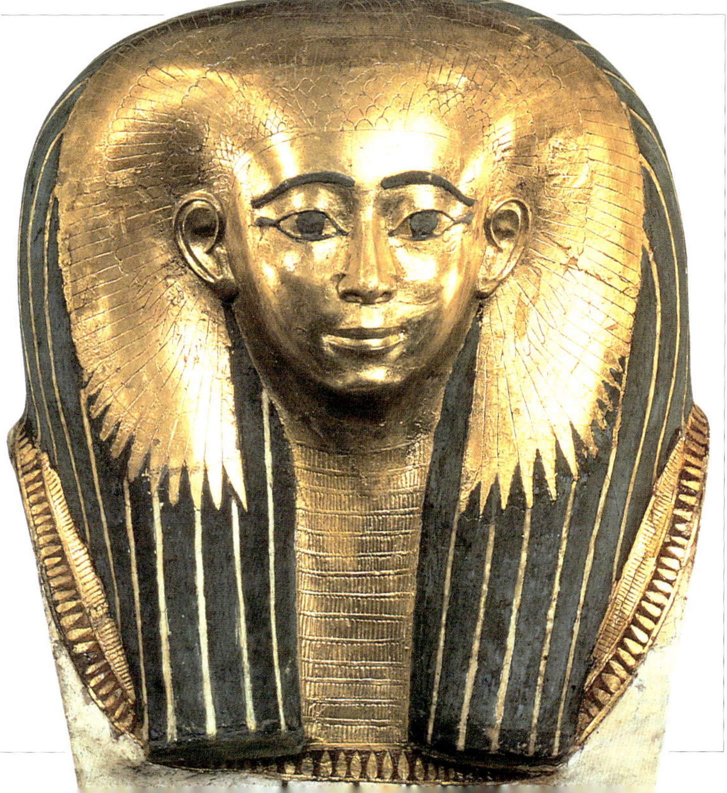

Inner Sarcophagus of Merymose

Eighteenth Dynasty, *c.*1370 BC

Anthropoid coffins of stone were provided for high-ranking officials during the New Kingdom, and were also made for kings (that of Sety I in Sir John Soane's Museum, London, is the finest surviving example). One of the first individuals to be buried in such a coffin was Merymose, Viceroy of Nubia in the reign of Amenhotep III. His tomb at Thebes contained an elaborate set of three mummiform sarcophagi nested one within the other: an outer one of red granite and two smaller ones of grey granite, decorated with images and hieroglyphic texts derived from those of contemporary wooden coffins. Ancient tomb robbers broke Merymose's sarcophagi into pieces, but many fragments have survived. The face of the innermost coffin, fortunately preserved intact, is a superb piece of sculpture, representing the dead man wearing the tripartite wig and a short beard.

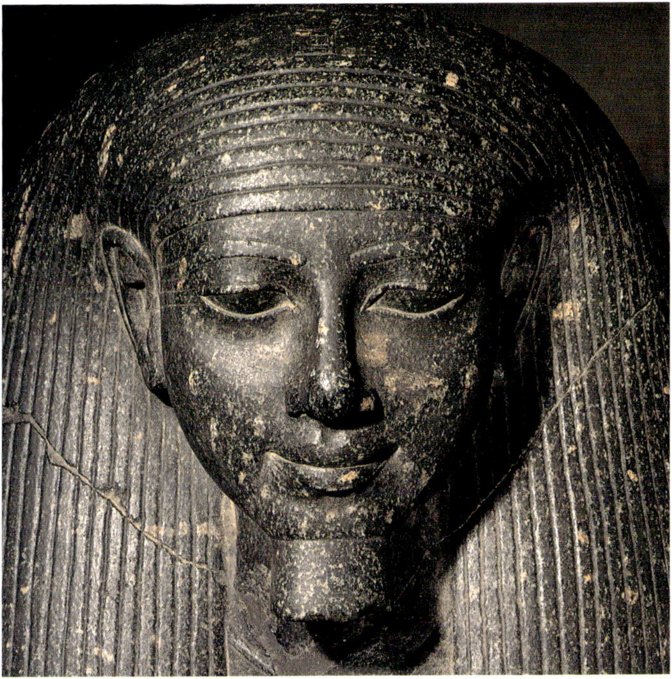

Mummy Mask
Late Eighteenth Dynasty,
c.1400-1300 BC

This attractive and lifelike mask was probably made for the mummy of a woman, and can be dated on stylistic grounds to the late Eighteenth Dynasty. It is made from the wood of the sycamore fig, a tree native to Egypt which was extensively used in the manufacture of funerary equipment, particularly coffins. The front and rear were carved as separate pieces, before being joined together, coated with plaster and painted. The outer rows of the collar are composed of lotus petals and fruits or berries. Such floral garlands were worn at feasts held in honour of the dead, and actual examples used at the funeral of Tutankhamun have been discovered in the Valley of the Kings. Like the components of the collar, the perforations in the ear-lobes have been carefully delineated.

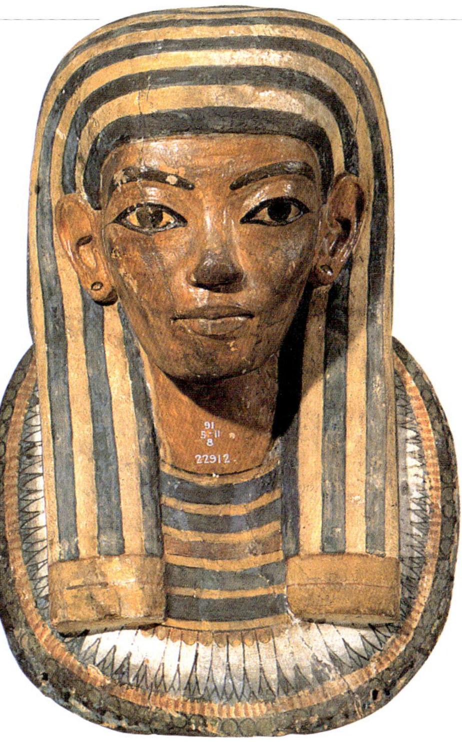
91
5-11
8
22912.

Mummy-Board of Ankhefenmut

Twenty-First Dynasty, *c.*1069-945 BC

The well-to-do citizen of Thebes in the Twenty-first Dynasty would expect his mummy to rest in a burial-ensemble comprising two anthropoid coffins, nested one inside the other. Over the corpse itself was placed a mummy-board, which resembled the lids of the outer and inner coffins and took the place of a wooden or cartonnage mask. The mummy-board of the priest Ankhefenmut from Deir el-Bahri illustrates the typical features of these objects – the tripartite wig (here rather narrow in order to fit comfortably inside the inner coffin), the elaborate festal collar and the decorative fillet. The facial features, and particularly the internal anatomy of the ears, have been carefully reproduced. The three red lines painted on the throat are the artist's shorthand for rolls of fat – a metaphor in Egyptian iconography for the possession of a privileged existence, distinguished by a rich and abundant diet and exemption from hard physical labour.

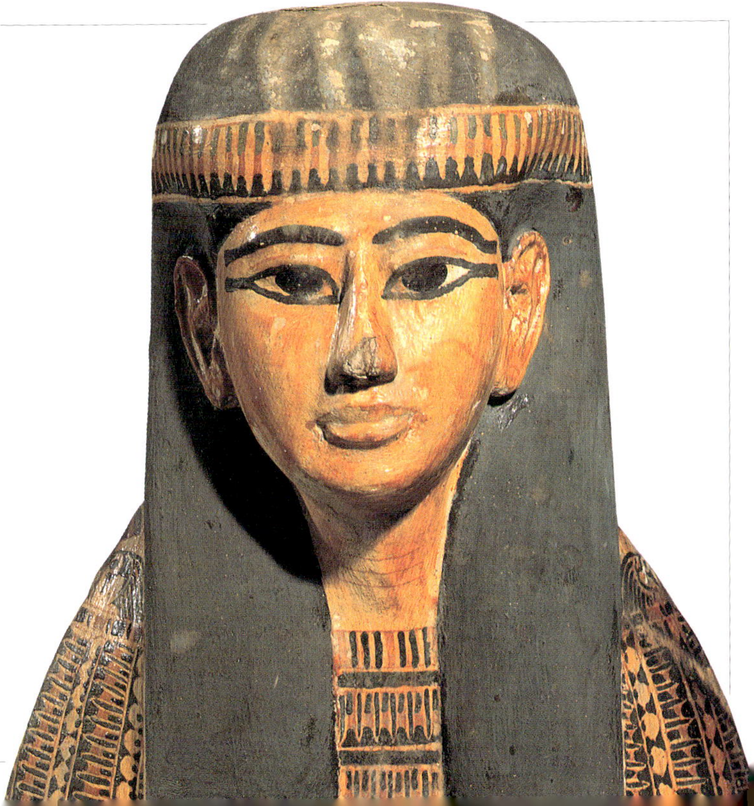

Lid of the Coffin of Ta-ahuti

Twenty-First Dynasty, *c*.1069-945 BC

This coffin was discovered in 1891 in a large rock-cut tomb at Deir el-Bahri, known as the 'Cache of the Priests of Amun'. The tomb, which had fortunately escaped robbery, contained the mummies of 153 members of the clergy of the god Amun, gathered together by the Theban authorities at the end of the Twenty-first Dynasty. 101 of the bodies possessed two coffins. In the course of transferring the mummies from their original resting-places to the cache, the outer and inner coffins seem to have been separated, and in a number of instances were never reunited. This outer coffin bears the name of a lady, Ta-ahuti, but the inner case that it contained was inscribed for another person named Tawesertempernesu. Ta-ahuti's own inner coffin and her mummy were never identified; possibly they had been lost or destroyed by robbers, and her surviving outer coffin was recycled for Tawesertempernesu.

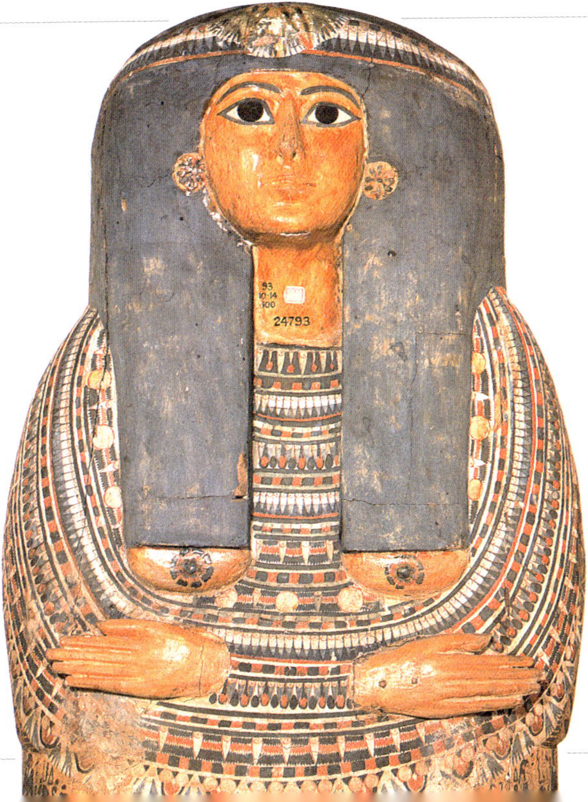
93
10-14
100
24793

Coffin of an Unnamed Woman

Twenty-First Dynasty, *c.*1069-945 BC

Many early anthropoid coffins were intended to serve as an idealised image of the deceased, and represent them appropriately adorned with funerary trappings. The faces of such coffins are usually framed by the formal striped wig associated with divinities. In the Nineteenth and Twentieth Dynasties (*c.*1295-1069 BC), however, coffins representing the deceased in the costume of daily life were popular. Although this type was abandoned in the Twenty-first Dynasty, the elaborate headgear of women's coffins constituted a partial survival of the tradition. This unidentified woman wears a heavy wig of a type commonly seen on festal occasions. New Kingdom tomb paintings show that fillets of lotus petals were tied around the brows, and bunches of lotus flowers laid over the top of the wig. These have been faithfully reproduced by the artist, as have the large ornamental ear-studs and decorative hair bands.

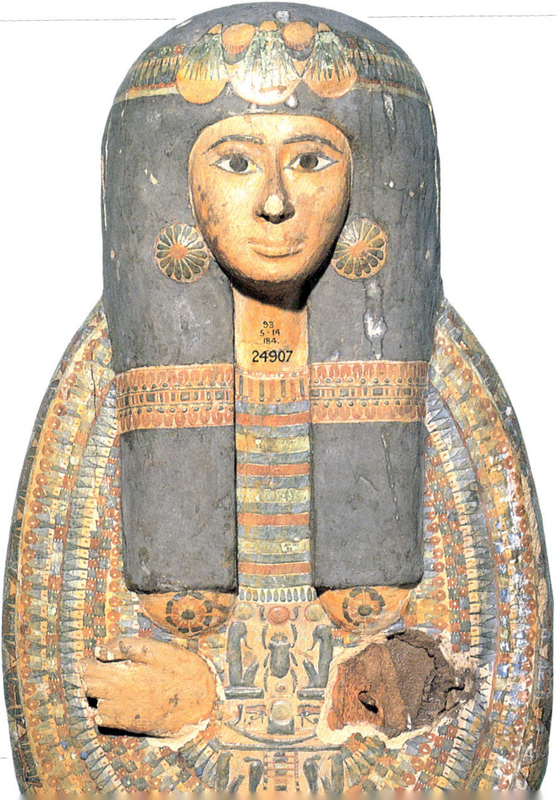
93
5 · 14
184.
24907

The Sunrise: Coffin of Djedhorefankh

Early Twenty-Second Dynasty, *c.*945-900 BC

The rising sun symbolised for the ancient Egyptians the renewal of life, and was represented in a variety of religious images. In one of the commonest, the solar disc is propelled forward by the scarab beetle, itself regarded as a manifestation of the newly risen sun. In this scene, on the interior of a richly painted coffin from Thebes, the sunrise takes place beneath the vault of heaven, represented as a blue arc framing the entire scene. Protective serpents envelop the solar disc, and the goddesses Isis and Nephthys welcome it with libations, food offerings and the burning of incense.

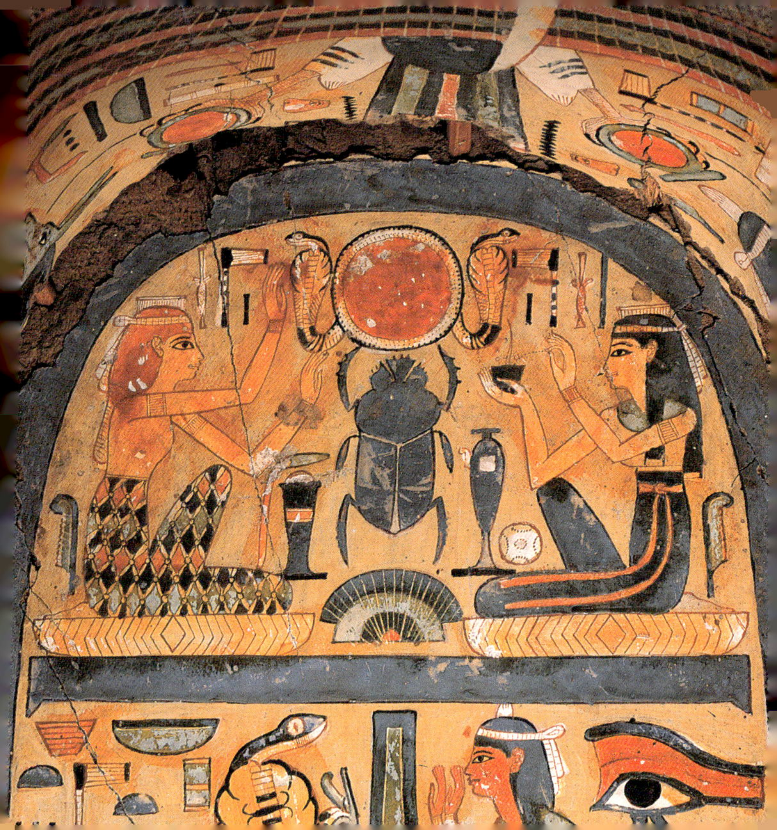

Head of the Coffin of Hor

Twenty-Second Dynasty, *c.*945-715 BC

For the ancient Egyptians, the decomposition and dismembering of the corpse was to be avoided at all costs, and special attention was devoted to ensuring the preservation of the head, regarded as the most important part of the body. Cartonnage mummy masks, introduced around 2200 BC, could serve as substitutes for the head, and the anthropoid mummy cases which developed from the masks always incorporated a representation of the head, even when other bodily features such as the arms and hands were omitted. The faces of the coffins are, like the majority of Egyptian funerary images, idealised, and are in no sense portraits of the owner. The brilliant, red-painted face of this coffin, then, represents the temple incense-bearer Hor as he wished to appear in the afterlife – eternally young and physically perfect.

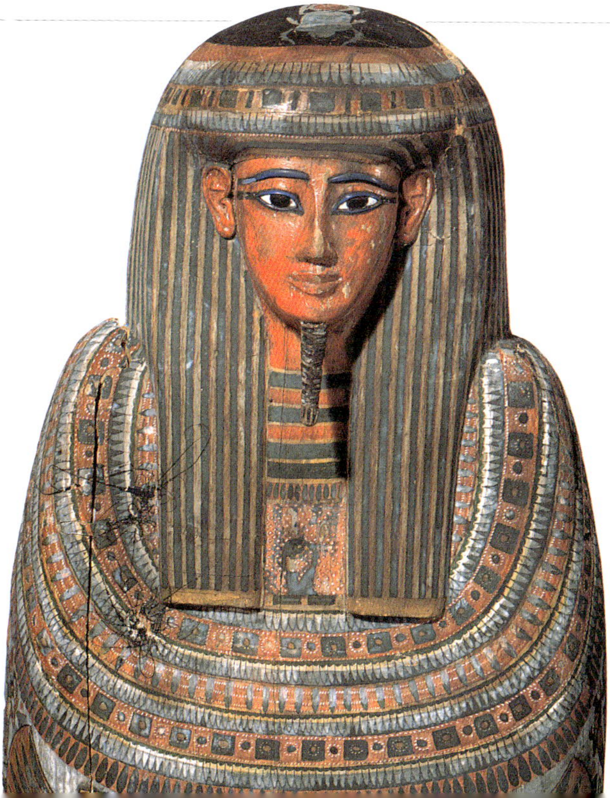

Interior of the Coffin of Hor

Twenty-Second Dynasty, *c.*945-715 BC

Boldly painted on the inside of the coffin lid, this figure of a mummiform falcon-headed god was intended to protect the body lying beneath it and to assist in the dead man's resurrection. The hieroglyphic inscription down the right-hand side is the beginning of a standard request for funerary offerings, addressed to Osiris, 'Lord of Ta-djeser'. In the image, however, attributes of Osiris are mingled with those of other deities; the figure is probably intended to represent Ptah-Sokar-Osiris, a composite funerary deity. He is equipped with the royal crook and 'flail' sceptres, and behind him is the hieroglyphic sign for 'West', the region of the dead. The god's feet rest on a group of bows – a standard convention in Egyptian art to symbolise triumph over enemies or hostile forces. In this way the deceased was assured of protection from the many dangers which were believed to threaten his safe passage into the next life.

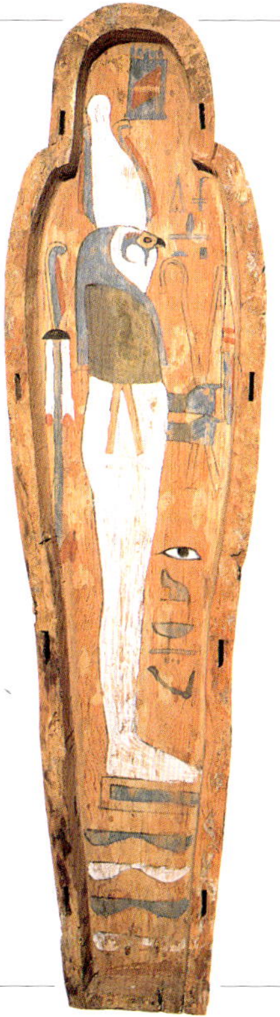

Mummy of Tjentmutengebtiu

Early Twenty-Second Dynasty, *c.*900 BC

The mummy of Tjentmutengebtiu, daughter of the priest of Amun, Khonsmose, was enclosed in an enveloping body-case made of cartonnage. Such coffins were in widespread use in Egypt during the ninth and eighth centuries BC, and were elaborately decorated with texts and images relating to rebirth and the afterlife. Tjentmutengebtiu's mummy has

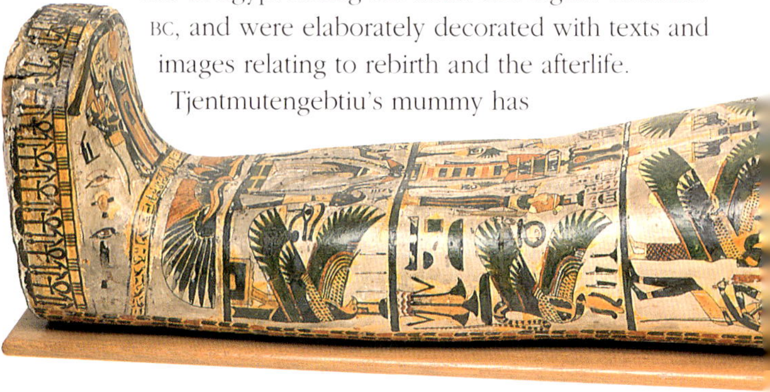

never been removed from her cartonnage, but details of what lies inside have been obtained by computer-assisted tomography (CAT scanning). This method has revealed the presence of amulets and artificial eyes within the wrappings, and has enabled the lady's age to be estimated at between 19 and 23 years, based on high-resolution images of her wisdom-teeth, an important guide to age at death.

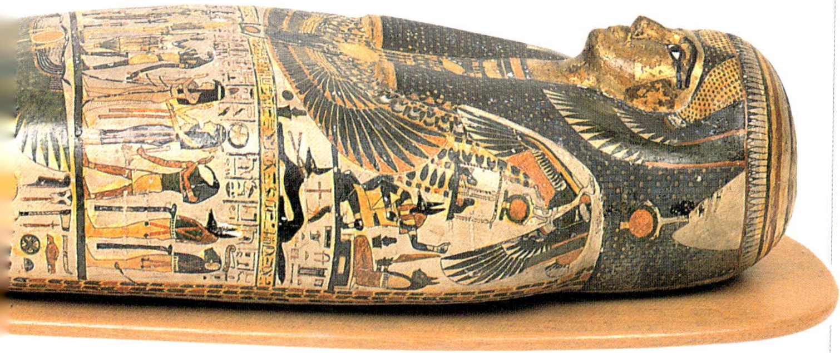

Inner Coffin of Takhebkhenem

Twenty-Fifth Dynasty, *c.*680 BC

The coffin – whether rectangular or mummiform – could symbolically represent the universe in which the deceased was to be resurrected, and this function was often reflected in the decoration applied to the interior surfaces. The lid was associated with the heavens, and hence was adorned with a depiction of the sky-goddess Nut, extending herself in an eloquent gesture of protection over the mummy within. Her name is written in hieroglyphs above her head, and she is shown full-face, a type of depiction rarely employed by Egyptian artists. The case was linked with the concept of the terrestrial Underworld, ruled over by Osiris, and it is his emblem, the *Djed*-pillar, which is painted there. The pillar springs forth from the *Tit*, or 'girdle of Isis', and, above, the radiant solar disc is supported by the arms of Nun, personification of the primeval waters. These arms, in turn, emerge from the *ankh*, the hieroglyphic sign for 'life'.

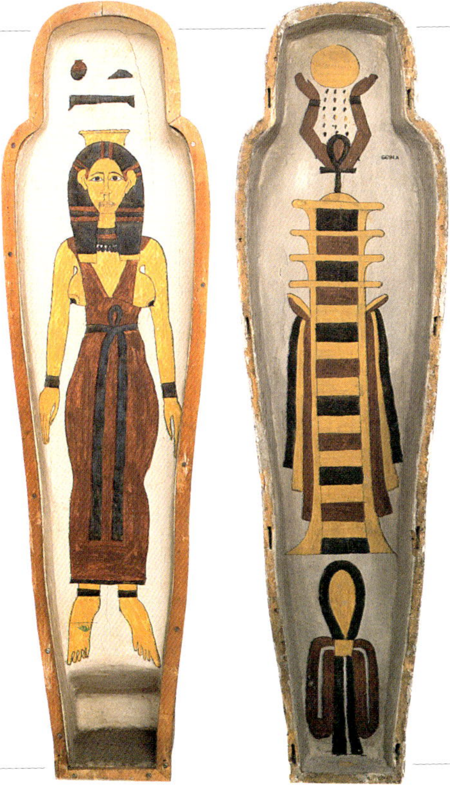

Lid of the Coffin of Pasenhor

Twenty-Fifth Dynasty, *c*.700 BC

This beautiful example of the ancient Egyptian painter's craft was made for Pasenhor, a member of the Meshwesh – one of numerous Libyan groups who exercised enormous influence over Egypt during the Third Intermediate Period. Despite his non-Egyptian origins, the decoration of Pasenhor's coffin shows that he had thoroughly absorbed the religious attitudes of his adopted land. Much of the pictorial and textual matter is drawn from Chapter 125 of the *Book of the Dead*. This chapter concerns the posthumous judgement, a kind of 'character assessment' designed to vindicate the dead man before the divine tribunal presided over by Osiris, to prove his worthiness to enter the hereafter. The most important part of this test was the weighing of the deceased's heart in a balance, an episode depicted on the right of the band of figured scenes on the breast.

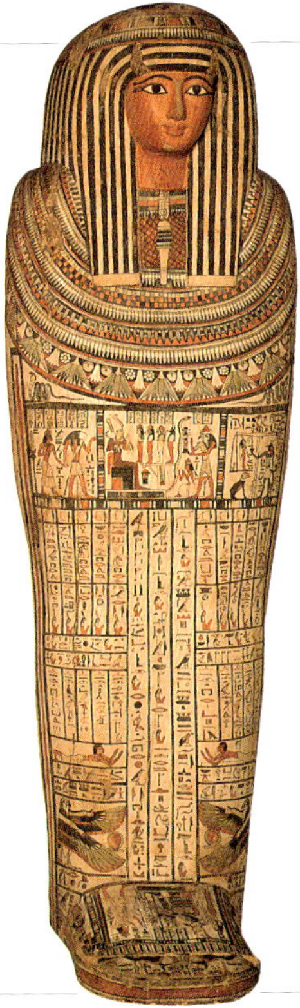

Coffin of Djedmontefankh

Late Twenty-Fifth or Early Twenty-Sixth Dynasty, *c.*680-650 BC

The inscriptions on this wooden coffin from Thebes reveal that its owner, Djedmontefankh, was a temple door-keeper, and that his father Ikesenuita held the same title. He was thus a man of middle rank, and this is

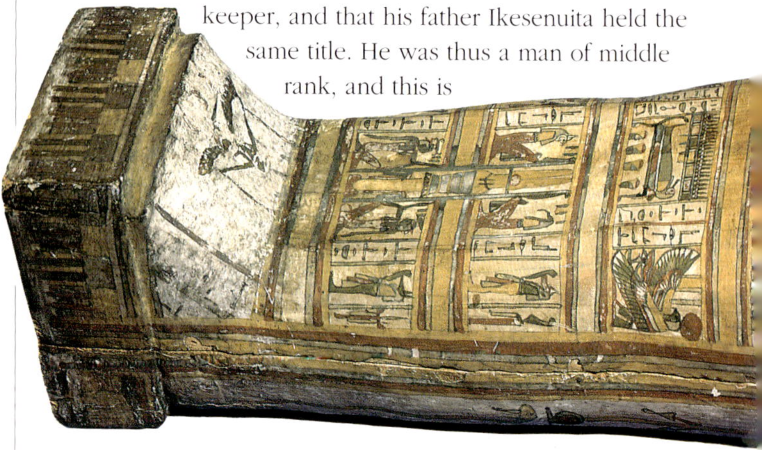

reflected in the workmanship and decoration of his coffin, which is competent but not outstanding. The inscriptions are limited to a few common formulae requesting offerings, and the scenes which occupy the compartments are standardised images: the weighing of the dead man's heart in the balance of judgement, the mummy lying on a bier, and various protective deities including Nut and Isis.

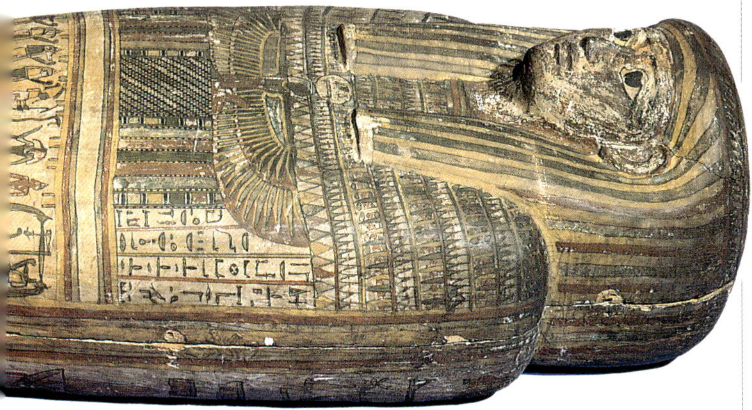

Basalt Sarcophagus Lid of Sasobek

Twenty-Sixth Dynasty, 664-525 BC

From the Twenty-fifth Dynasty to the Ptolemaic Period, many stone sarcophagi of anthropoid shape were made, particularly for persons of high rank. This example, one of the finest of its type, was made for a man named Sasobek, who held office as Vizier (chief minister) and priest of the Memphite god Ptah in the early years of the Twenty-sixth Dynasty. In the elegant simplicity of its design it imitates closely the wooden coffins of the period. Sasobek wears the striped tripartite wig and curled ceremonial beard associated with deities – visible signs that through resurrection he has attained the status of divinity. His body is completely enveloped in a shroud, from which only his hands emerge, crossed on the breast. He grasps the *Djed*-pillar and the *Tit*, emblems associated with Osiris and Isis.

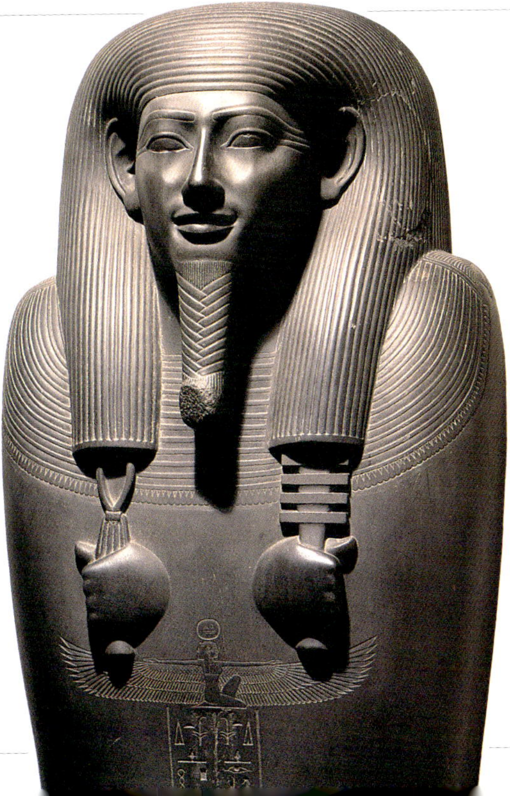

Head of the Mummy of Irthorru

Twenty-Sixth Dynasty, *c.*600 BC

Irthorru, a priest at the important provincial town of Akhmim in Upper Egypt, was buried in a painted anthropoid coffin of wood, and his mummy was adorned with a fine gilded mask and a network of blue-faience tubular beads. Apart from superficial damage to the mask and wrappings, his mummy is in good condition. X-rays have revealed that Irthorru died in middle-age; he still had all his teeth, and his skeleton shows no signs of fractures or dislocations. Amulets, including a falcon-shaped pectoral ornament, have been detected within the wrappings, and packing material has been observed in the thorax.

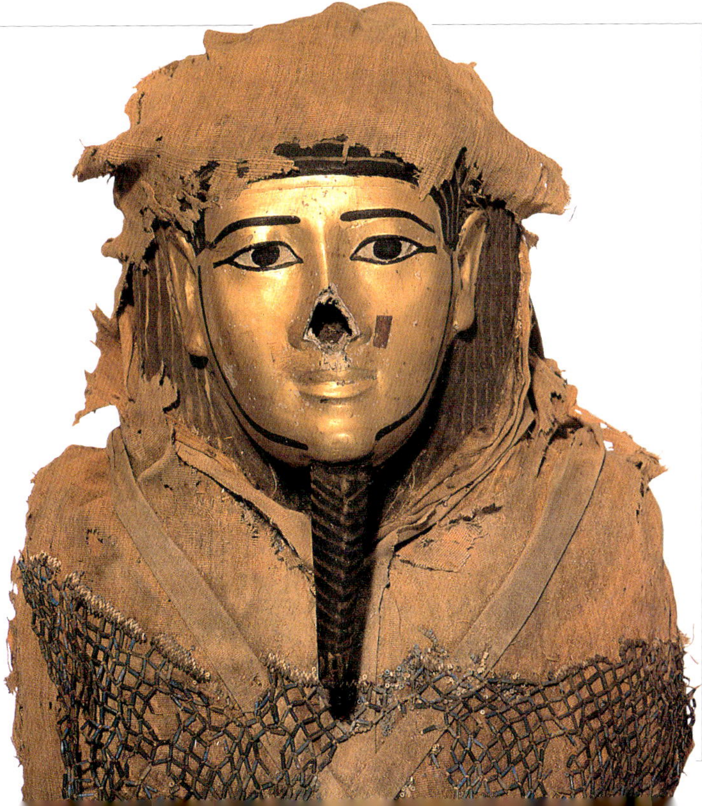

Coffin of Itineb

Twenty-Sixth Dynasty, 664-525 BC

The myth of Osiris was crucial to ancient Egyptian concepts of life after death. Murdered by his brother Seth and subsequently restored to life, Osiris symbolised for all Egyptians the prospect of survival beyond the grave. He was also a vegetation-god, linked with the new growth of plants (a metaphor for rebirth), and because of this was frequently depicted with green skin. An individual's hopes of resurrection depended to a large extent on a close identification with Osiris, and to this end, the deceased was regularly referred to as 'the Osiris X'. Sometimes this association was emphasised by colouring the face-mask of the coffin green. This example, belonging to a man named Itineb, probably comes from Saqqara. Below the formal collar are painted the winged goddess Nut, a scene showing the judgement of the deceased before Osiris, and twenty small vignettes in each of which Itineb adores a different deity.

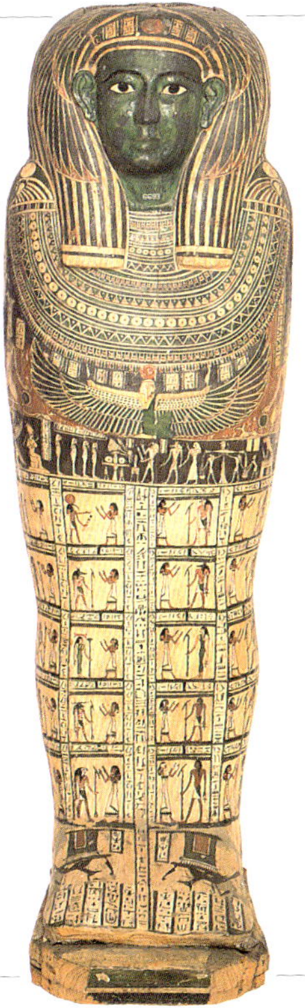

Mummy Mask of Hornedjitef

Ptolemaic Period, Third century BC

The custom of placing a mask over the mummy's head fell out of widespread use after the New Kingdom (*c*.1550-1069 BC), but enjoyed a revival during the Ptolemaic and Roman periods (after 305 BC). One of the earliest firmly dated examples from this era is the well-preserved cartonnage mask of the priest Hornedjitef, who was buried at Thebes, probably in the reign of Ptolemy III (246-222 BC). The striped tripartite wig, gilded face and elaborate collar are all traditional features, which had appeared on masks centuries earlier, but religious scenes and texts were now added, to emphasise the mask's magical capacity to promote the divinisation and resurrection of its owner. Images of gods and goddesses appear on the sides and back, while on the top of the head is an elaborate representation of the sunrise.

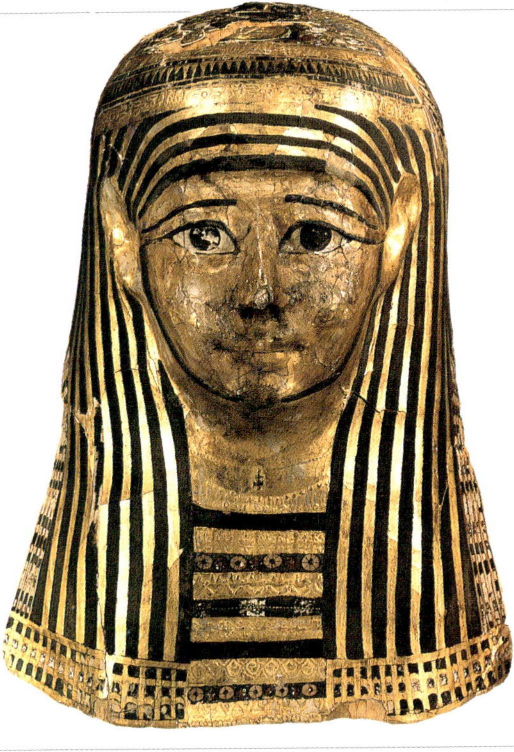

Cartonnage Mummy Mask

Ptolemaic Period, 305-30 BC

In the Ptolemaic Period special attention was devoted to the external appearance of the mummy (though the bodies within the wrappings were often poorly embalmed and, as X-rays have demonstrated, were frequently incomplete or damaged). A major feature of this fashion in embellishing the exterior was the reintroduction of the cartonnage mask as a regular element of the mummy's trappings. Besides the mask, the wrappings were adorned with cartonnage pectorals, body-plaques and footcases, brightly painted with figures of deities. Many of these trappings were prefabricated and provide no indication of the identity or even of the sex of the owner. This mask, from a mummy discovered at Atfih in Middle Egypt, is typical of many in the bland idealism of its facial features and almost certainly represents a ready-made piece, intended to be purchased 'off the shelf'.

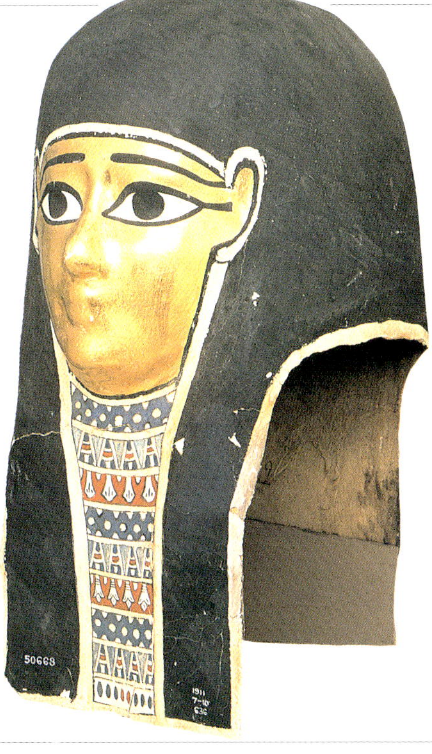
50668
1911

Mummy of a Youth With Portrait Panel

Roman Period, Early Second Century AD

This mummy of a young man has the intricate patterned bandaging and painted panel-portrait characteristic of the finer burials of the Roman Period. The portrait is painted on wood in encaustic – a technique in which beeswax was used as a medium to give the finished image added luminosity and durability. The artist's bold treatment of his subject and skilful handling of light and shade lend the panel an admirably lifelike appearance. Although many panels of this type have been found, particularly at Hawara in the Faiyum (the source of this specimen), it remains unclear to what extent they are actual likenesses of the deceased. In this case, the impression of the subject's age conveyed by the portrait is borne out by X-rays of the body, which is that of an adolescent. Radiography also shows that the bones are in great disorder, suggesting that decomposition may have been already far advanced when the embalmers began work.

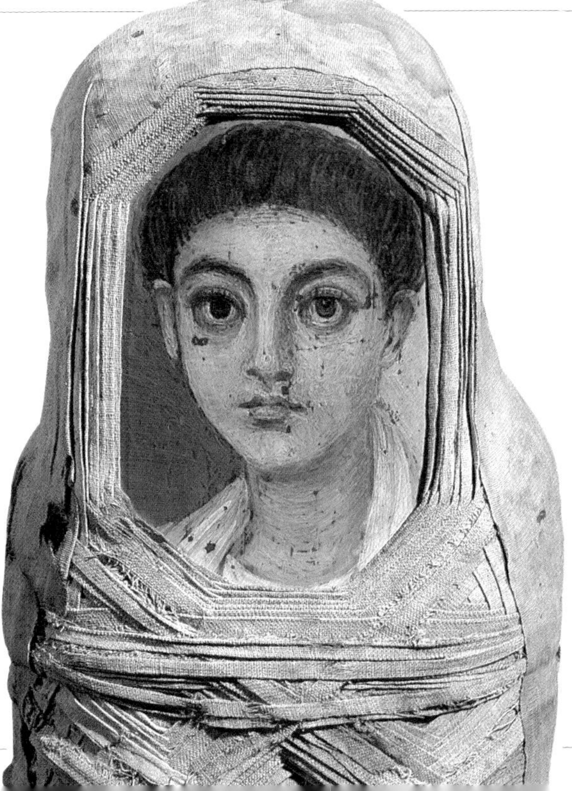

Gilded Cartonnage Mummy Mask of Syros

Roman Period, Late First Century AD

Cartonnage headpieces remained popular into the Roman Period, continuing in use alongside the encaustic panel-portraits. This specimen belonged to a person named Syros (his name is written on the mask in Greek characters). Syros was buried at Hawara, a cemetery serving the city of Arsinoe, together with other family members whose bodies were likewise sumptuously adorned. The headdress is similar in design to those of Ptolemaic and earlier masks, and the subject matter of the painted scenes – the human-headed *Ba* bird, the mummy on a lion-bier and the protective serpent deities – are purely pharaonic. The winged sphinxes, however, reveal Classical influence. The lively appearance of the face derives partly from the careful modelling and is enhanced by the realistic eyes. The pupils are a composite of differently coloured glass set in crystalline limestone, and mounted in copper alloy settings.

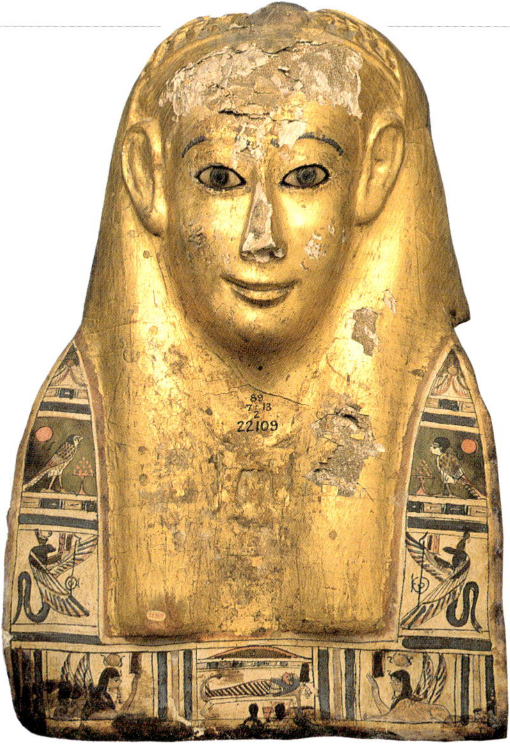
89
7 13
2
22109

Mummified Jackal

Roman Period, after 30 BC

Animals were frequently the focus of worship by the ancient Egyptians, chiefly through their association with particular deities, rather than as gods in their own right. In the earlier phases of the Pharaonic Period a single animal was chosen as the earthly representative of the god. It lived in the temple precinct, enjoyed privileged living conditions, and was mummified after its death. From the Late Period to the Roman Period, large numbers of sacred animals and birds were kept in temple enclosures. They were deliberately killed and mummified, so that they could be purchased by pilgrims for presentation as votive offerings to the appropriate god or goddess. This small mummified jackal of the Roman Period exemplifies a common custom of the time, by which the mummy is wrapped in the manner of a human body, with bandages arranged in an intricate pattern and with an idealised representation of the creature's head.

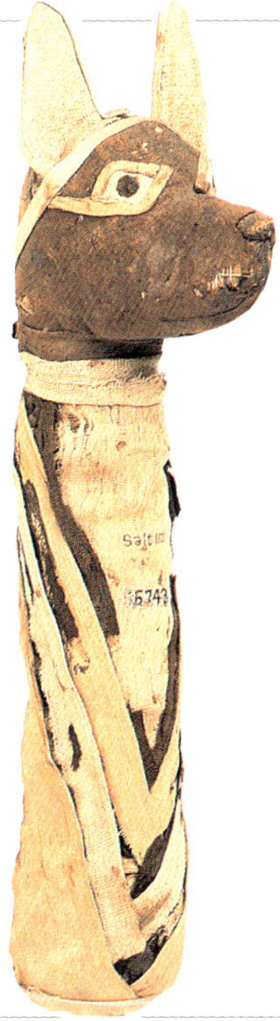
Salt

Accession numbers of objects illustrated

Page	
4	EA 6660
9	EA 32751
10	EA 6697
13	EA 46631
15	EA 55315
17	EA 6652
19	EA 29770
21	EA 1001
23	EA 22912
25	EA 24797
27	EA 24793
29	EA 24907
31	EA 22900
33	EA 6659
35	EA 6659
36	EA 22939
39	EA 6691
41	EA 24906
42	EA 25256
45	EA 17
47	EA 20745
49	EA 6693
51	EA 6679
53	EA 50668
55	EA 13595
57	EA 22109
59	EA 6743

First published in 1996 by British Museum Press
A division of The British Museum Company Ltd
46 Bloomsbury Street, London WC1B 3QQ

A catalogue record for this book is available from the British Library

ISBN 0-7141-2101-0

Text by John Taylor
Photography by British Museum Photographic Service
Designed by Butterworth Design

Typeset in Garamond
Manufactured in China
by Imago Publishing Ltd

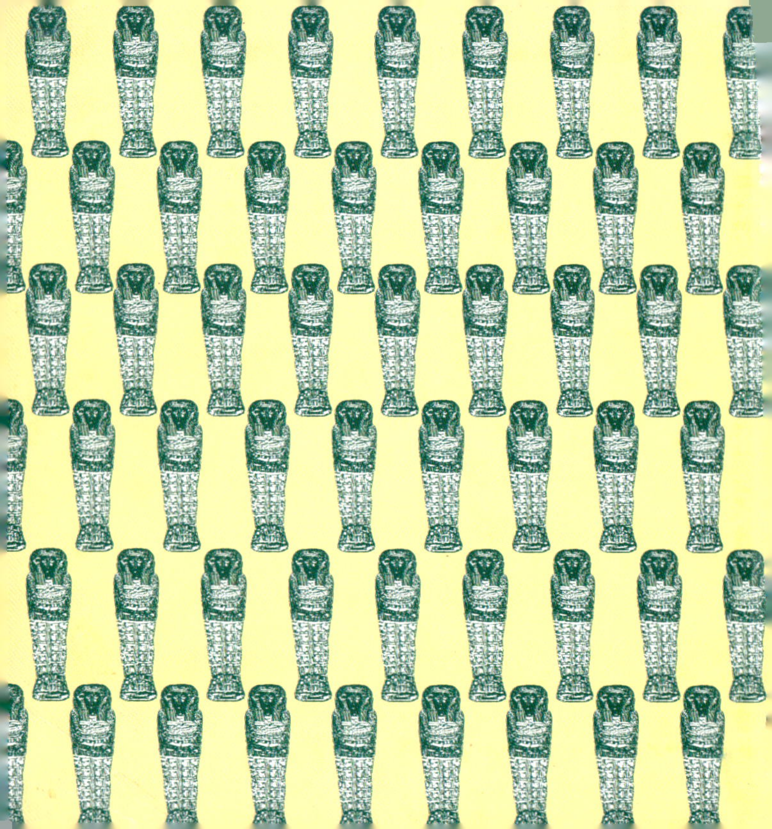